Seasons of Marriage

written and illustrated by
Emily Williams- Wheeler.

Adventure Publications
Cambridge, Minnesota

Published by
Adventure Publications, Inc.
P.O. Box 269
Cambridge, MN 55008

ISBN 1-885061-70-6

For you.

It begins

as a diamond in the rough.

Then come fragrant offerings,

a sweet rendez-vous,

and wishing on the same star.

There are endless days
that float along

and an awkward giggle or two.

Two moving together as one

to the moment
we've been waiting for.

It begins again, a renaissance,

a world filled up by two,

then, wonderfully, three.

Precious moments, precious firsts.

We savor three together;

but still find time for two.

We capture highlights

and gather memories

until the nest empties

and other nests are made.

Home alone!

for a moonlight serenade.

The road goes on,

the cycle of love continues,

as the embers still burn brightly

for you, the night, and the music.

For more information

on books by
Emily Williams-Wheeler,
contact your local
gift / book store or
Adventure Publications
1·800·678·7006.